James J. H. Gregory

Carrots, Mangold Wurtzels and Sugar Beets

James J. H. Gregory

Carrots, Mangold Wurtzels and Sugar Beets

ISBN/EAN: 9783337144654

Printed in Europe, USA, Canada, Australia, Japan

Cover: Foto ©Andreas Hilbeck / pixelio.de

More available books at **www.hansebooks.com**

CARROTS,

MANGOLD WURTZELS

AND

SUGAR BEETS.

———

HOW TO RAISE THEM, HOW TO KEEP THEM AND HOW TO FEED THEM.

By JAMES J. H. GREGORY,

AUTHOR OF "ONION RAISING," "CABBAGE RAISING," &C.

———

MARBLEHEAD, MASS :

N. ALLEN LINDSEY & CO.,

1877.

CARROTS.

THE ARGUMENT FOR THE RAISING OF ROOTS.

The fact that the most progressive and successful farmers in the dairy districts, where the prices received for the products of the dairy stimulates to the highest enterprise, are raisers of roots, (by which I now more especially refer to Carrots or Mangold Wurtzel) in about the same degree as they are pecuniarily successful, is in itself a great practical argument for root culture.

In nutritious value roots compare with hay in about the average proportion of one to three. If now we consider that thirty-four tons of Swedes, nearly forty tons of Carrots and seventy-four tons of Mangold roots have been raised in Massachusetts, to the acre, and that to each of these crops should be added at least 15 per cent. for the fodder value of the yield of leaves, which were not included in these estimates, we have a demonstration of how immensely more is the nourishment that can be obtained from an acre of roots than from an acre in hay. Such an immense increase in the nourishing products of the farm, if fed on the premises as it should be, unless the farmer is so located that he can buy manure cheaper than he can make it, means a great increase in the manure products, and consequently a great increase in the crops,—so that it has been wisely said, root culture lies at the basis of good husbandry.

Carrots and Mangolds are subject to but few diseases. In discussing the nutritious value, chemists differ somewhat, according as they measure this by the nitrogen they contain, their per cent. of dry matter or sugar, but they agree in ranking them much superior to the early varieties of turnip and somewhat superior to the Ruta Baga or Swede class, particularly when fed to full grown cattle. Prof. Johnson ranks Carrots with Cabbage when fed to oxen, for nourishment, and experiments appear to have proved that when equal measures of each are fed, Mangolds will give a greater increase of milk than potatoes, by about a third. For some reason not fully understood, (perhaps the depth they penetrate the soil has something to do with it ;) Onions will do better after Carrots than after any other crop, the yield being larger, the bulb handsomer, while the crop will bottom down earlier and better. Unlike Turnips or Swedes, with high manuring the crop can be profitably grown for years on the same piece of land. Swine prefer Mangolds to any root except the parsnip, and both in this country and in England store hogs, weighing from 125 lbs. and upwards have been carried through the winter in fine condition, when fed wholly on raw Sugar Beets or Mangolds. Chemists rank Carrots, when compared with oats, with reference to their fat and flesh forming qualities as 1 to 5.

Not only have roots a value in themselves as food, but they have a special office, taking to a large degree the place of grass and preventing the constipation that dry feed sometimes causes. While practice proves that they should not be relied upon to entirely supersede hay or grain, still they increase the value of either of these to a large degree ; and for slow working stock they may be fed with profit in place of from a third to half the grain usually given. Carrots add not only to the richness of the color, but also to the quality of the milk, while the flavor of the butter made from such milk is improved. Carrots fed in moderate quantities to horses give additional gloss to their hairy coats, and have not only a medicinal value when given to such as have been over-grained, but aid them in digesting grain, as may be seen in the dung of horses fed on oats with Carrots, and that of those fed on oats without Carrots. When cooked they are sometimes fed to poultry, and either cooked or raw to swine. In the family economy they have their place, particularly when young and fresh, while in Europe they enter largely into the composition of the well-known vegetable soups of the French.

THE CARROT.

"The Carrot," (*Daucus Carota*) says Burr in his "Field and Garden Vegetables of America," a book worthy a place in every farmer's library,—"in its cultivated state is a half-hardy biennial. It is indigenous to some parts of Great Britian, generally growing in chalky or sandy soil, and to some extent has become naturalized in this country; being found in gravelly pastures and mowing fields, and occasionally by roadsides, in loose places, where the surface has been disturbed or removed. In its native state the root is small, slender and fibrous or woody, of no value, and even of questionable properties as an article of food."

The average result of several analyses of the Carrot as given by Dr. Voelcker, is as follows:—

Water,   -   -   -   -   -   -   87.0
Albuminous Compounds,   -   -   -   -   .7
Fat,   -   -   .   -   .   -   .2
Pectine,   -   -   -   -   -   1.2

Cellular Fiber,	-	-	-	•	•	3.5
Sugar,	-	-	-	-	-	6.5
Ash,	-	-	-	-	-	.9

THE LOCATION AND SOIL.

It is important in selecting a location for the Carrot bed that the land should be nearly level, as otherwise the seed will be liable to wash out after heavy showers, and the plants while young be either washed out or covered with soil and killed. The land should be clear of all large rocks, and as far as possible of all stones up to the size of a hen's egg. The presence of large rocks 'in place,' as the geologists say, would interfere with the continuity of the rows, while the loose stones are not only always in the way while raking and planting the bed, but are also in the way of the slide or wheel hoes which are apt to knock them against the young plants to their injury. It is important that the piece of ground selected for a crop that will require so much manure and labor should have every advantage possible in its favor; it should not only be level and comparatively free from stones, but if possible should have been previously under high cultivation, that it may come to Carrots when in high condition.

The best soil, particularly for the Long Orange variety, is a loam mellow to the depth of two feet or more. On such soil the Carrot will perfect itself, growing straight and altogether beautiful to look upon, as they stretch from side to side of the bushel boxes. On some market gardens near critical markets, farmers find it for their interest to ascertain by actual experiment on what part of their grounds the root will grow longest and straightest, and when such plot is found make it a permanent bed. If the soil does not naturally grow a long carrot and they are desired, the end may be attained by trenching deep and adding sand. The difference

in the shape of the Long Orange, when grown on a deep
mellow loam, and on a heavy soil with a compact sub-soil, is
so remarkable that it would be almost impossible to make an
inexperienced person believe each lot was from the same
seed,—those grown on the heavy soil, resting on a compact sub-soil, oftentimes so closely resembling the Intermediate varieties as not to be distinguished from them.
Though the course is not on the whole to be advised, yet
Carrots can be raised on freshly turned sod. Such land will
be very free from weeds, and by making good use of the
wheel harrow, and applying manure in a very fine state,
should the season be a moist one, fair crops may be raised.
Reclaimed meadows in a good state of cultivation, which
are well-drained to the depth of thirty inches, will oftentimes
grow crops, large in bulk, but the individual roots are oftentimes inclined to "sprangle," and unless such meadows
have been well drained, and liberally covered with sand or
gravelly loam, they are apt to be spongy and inferior. When
grown on land inclining to clay, they are apt to be small and
woody in structure ; still, such land, if made friable by good
underdraining and the application of sand may be made
fair carrot ground.

THE MANURE AND ITS APPLICATION.

All root crops delight in most liberal manuring and the
highest of cultivation.   Carrots are no exception to this rule.
With every crop, other conditions being equal, *it is the last
half of the manure gives the profits;* and the more costly the
cultivation required the more important it is that this golden
fact be borne in mind. Though chemical analysis shows difference in the composition of all roots, and that there is
therefore an office for special manures, yet their general
composition is so nearly alike, and animal manures, most of

which contain in greater or less proportion, all the elements required, are so difficult to handle in just the proportions that would be required from the chemical standpoint, particularly when we consider that soils on which root crops are grown are usually rich in manures, varying in their chemical constituents, left over from former crops ;—for this reason I treat of manure by the cord and with reference to its comparative strength, bulk for bulk, rather than of its chemical elements.

Eight cords of good stable manure, nine cords of a compost made of one part night soil to two parts muck or loam ; twelve cords of a compost made of one-third fish waste, by which I mean the heads and back-bones of the fisheries, and two-thirds soil; eight cords of muscle mud ; six or eight cords of rotten kelp—either of these applied to an acre of land in good condition by previous high cultivation would be sufficient tor a good crop of carrots. Other manures might be mentioned, but these will serve as a pretty good measure of value for any kind accessible to farmers in general. To produce a very large crop such as one would like to be able to point to when premium crops are called for, add from one quarter to one-half to the above quantities. The condition of the manure is a matter of importance ; the stable manure should be good ; not half bedding, not burnt, neither too coarse nor too new ; the night soil should have been well mixed with the soil in the compost heap, and have been pitched over twice with sufficient intervals between to allow it to develop some heat. The fish waste should be well decomposed, so well that all but the bones should have disappeared, and if these be very dark and brittle so much the better. The muscle mud should be rich in dead muscles. In all farming it is important that the manures applied should be in a fine condition mechanically, and particularly is this true of root crops. For the roots of all plants can take up only such parts of the manure as are dissolved in water, and the finer the manure is the more readily can water penetrate it.

A man who is unfortunately short of manures can materially increase the capacity of what he has by working it over until it is very fine.

When short of a supply of animal manure, guano and good phosphates, where the soil is already in good condition can be used with success, provided the season does not prove to be too dry a one. From eight hundred to a thousand pounds of Peruvian guano and from ten to fifteen hundred pounds of the best phosphates should be used. The famous fertilizer formulas of Prof. Stockbridge have generally done so well I should be willing to try them on an acre of Carrots, were I short of other manures.

There is another matter concerning our manures which requires attention; if they are too fresh or crude they will be apt, if applied to our long growing varieties, to drive the growth too much into the top of the Carrot, to the loss of the root, giving us tops to our knees with roots about the size of a hoe handle. It is important therefore, when used liberally, that they should be somewhat decomposed—that the mixtures should be *composts*, as far as the time will allow, and not mere mixtures. To the shorter varieties the crude manure may be applied with a degree of safety. Here let me note a fact that I think is of general application in farming, viz. :—that a style of manuring that will drive tall growing varieties of vegetable nearly all to tops or vine, with dwarf varieties of the same kind will work admirably. The Pea is a very good illustration; to get a good crop of Dwarf Tom Thumb, manure liberally, but the same quantity applied to the taller sorts would drive them excessively into vine at the expense of the crop.

Don't make your compost heap on the ground where the crop is to grow, for the result will be no crop where the heap stands. For the same reason it is bad policy to cart out any strong manure to stand on the land in heaps, no matter how small, over winter. There will be nothing lost by spreading the manure over the surface before the ground is frozen. In getting it into the soil, *keep it as near the surface as possible* without its interfering with the planting of the seed, bearing in mind the nitrogen, that element in manures, about the loss of which by evaporation there is much uncalled for anxiety tends to work down into the soil. If the manure is coarse it may be applied to the surface in the Fall and be deeply ploughed in, and in the Spring again brought to the surface by ploughing equally deep, having meanwhile received the benefits of frost and moisture.

In applying guano or the phosphates, keep them near the surface, scattering them broadcast and raking or harrowing in. It is best not to apply either of these all at once,—particularly is this true of guano. Apply about half at the time of sowing, and the remainder when the crop is about one-third grown—following it with the slide hoe, which will tend to work it in just under the surface. In applying guano and all similar fine manures in the Spring time, it is well to do so early in the day, as winds are apt to rise as the day advances, which seriously interfere with the economical application and even distribution. Both phosphates and guano tend to hasten the maturity of the crops to which they are applied. There is one condition that has a very important bearing on the cost of Carrots and all roots, viz. :—that both the ground and manure should be as free from all weed seed as possible. For this reason ground recently from the sod, the third year, provided it has been kept under a high state of cultivation, and such manures which from their very nature must be comparatively free from the seed of weeds, such as fish composts, night soil, or barn manure a year old, are to be preferred.

Dr. Voelcker gives the result of 10 analyses of the ashes of the root and 2 of the ashes of the leaves of the Carrot, and from these deduces the following as the number of pounds of mineral matter taken from an acre of land, by 10 tons of roots and 4 tons of tops.

Potash,	Soda,	Lime,	Phosphoric Acid,
116 lbs	86 lbs.	101 lbs.	31 lbs.
	Sulphuric Acid,		Chlorine,
	34 lbs.		31 lbs.

To those who desire to experiment with mineral manures this table will be interesting as showing the kinds and proportion of each needed. The potash is found in unleeched ashes, at the rate of 4 or 5 pounds to the bushel; or in the German Potash salts; the soda and chlorine in common salt, (chloride of sodium); lime in the common lime of the mason, the Phosphoric acid in the phosphates offered in the markets, and the Sulphuric acid in that directly or in common finely ground plaster, known by chemists as Sulphate of Lime.

I shall have occasion to present some very valuable suggestions of the learned Professor, under the head of "The Manure" in my article on Mangolds, to which they more especially apply.

The greatest single item in the cost of any crop is the manure, but this is an exceedingly varying element. Farmers near cities, and particularly if they also reside near the sea-coast, as an off-set for the greater cost of farming-land and expenses of living, have the advantages of a city market and special facilities for collecting manures, at a cost to them, much below the standard value of stable manure. Night soil to almost an unlimited extent, can be obtained for the cost of collecting it, while the waste material of the fisheries, Kelp, Rock Weed, Muscle Mud, Glue Waste, Sugar House Waste, and the products of the distilleries, these and other rich fertilizers can be procured at so low a figure, in proportion to their value, that root crops can be raised considerably cheaper than in farming districts not so favored. Many a man can be found in these favored districts who thinks he is making a good business at farming, yet could he but sell the manure he gathers so cheaply, at its market value, barn manure being the standard, he would make money by doing so and folding his arms the rest of the year. The fact is he is really losing money at farming ; but through his crops he is selling what cost him but a trifle, at a price, indeed, below its real value, but still so far in advance of cost as to leave a profit. Such a man does wisely in the course he pursues though he makes a mistake in the debtor and creditor side of the account, for it is most decidedly wiser to be at work than idle, though the result makes no difference in the dollars in a man's pocket.

PREPARING THE BED.

The great object here should be to get the soil thoroughly fine that the small, thread-like fibers, and the roots themselves, may waste the least possible vital power in permeating the earth in search of food, or in pushing downwards. The vitality wasted in this way is just so much taken from growth, and may make the sole difference between a good crop and a poor one. If it is necessary that the first ploughing should be a very deep one, better apply the manure, (as previously stated, the finer mechanical condition this is in the better) afterwards. Should the manure be to any degree coarse after spreading, run the brush or wheel harrow over it, one or both. This will also break up the clods and fine up the soil and incorporate the manure with it. If still at all lumpy, follow with a plank drag. Next plow shallow a few furrows, and have men, with wooden-toothed hand rakes, rake at right angles, pulling all coarse stones and lumps of earth and manure into the last furrow made. In brief, proceed to make as fine a seed bed as for onions.

If any one, depending on the apparent fineness of the surface, concludes to dispense with the final raking and let the work of the brush harrow answer, he will be apt to repent it before the season closes; should he try it let him be sure to double the quantity of seed planted in that portion of the land so treated. If the bed has its first ploughing early in the season, much of the weed seed will germinate before planting time and an occasional use of the cultivator will destroy many of the pests.

WHEN TO PLANT.

Some of our best farmers advocate planting about the middle of May, others equally successful in root culture claim that the middle of June is the best time. There are arguments for both early and late planting. In New England we usually have the weather sufficiently moist towards the close of May to insure the germination of the seed and protect the plants when they break ground, from "sun-scald." Those planted as late as the middle of June are more liable to be so affected by the dry weather usual at that period as not to vegetate as well; and should the heat be very great just after they push through the ground, sometimes in a single day nearly the entire crop will disappear by "sun-scald." But on the other hand, by planting late we about get rid of one weeding, assuming that the ground is stirred by the cultivator occasionally, up to the time of planting. Again, this brings the crop in full vigor in October, the month of all others most favorable for the growth of the root, and the Carrots being dug while the tops are in fair growing condition, keep better than when dug fully ripe. The argument

for late planting holds especially good for the Short Horn varieties, as these require a shorter time to mature than the long
kinds.   If the crop is planted too early, sometimes the roots
having matured, will attempt to push seed shoots ; when this
is so they will be found woody in their structure, with num-
berless thread-like roots while their quality and keeping properties are greatly injured.   This crop on rich land is sometimes planted as late as the first week in July, and with great
success, should the Fall prove exceptionably mild, yet, as a
rule, I would not recommend planting later than the middle of June.   If it so happens, from press of work, or the
dry weather, the farmer has to plant later than this, then by
all means let him confine himself to the earlier varieties.

THE SEED AND THE PLANTING OF IT.

To grow seed, medium-sized roots should be selected,
that are well-grown, straight and symmetrical, of a rich, dark
orange color, with a small, compact top.   Plant in rows three
and a half feet apart and fifteen inches in the row, the
crowns being on a level with the surface.   If the roots are
long they may be laid slanting in the furrows.   The best seed
will be from the two first cuttings, which will come from the
center of the main stock and of each side shoot.
The seed grows with a covering of small, short, stiff hairs,
which makes them adhere together ; these must be very thoroughly removed before the seed can be relied upon to flow
freely from the machine.   Much of foreign grown seed reaches
this country not properly cleaned.   To remove this furze,
either thrash the seed with the flail very thoroughly, when the
weather is quite cold and dry, or warm the seed slightly and
rub it with the hand against the wires of a sieve, of a right
degree of fineness to let the hairs fall through.   Either win-
now, or sink in water, to remove all impurities.   If sunk, be

careful to dry the seed at a very moderate temperature ; rubbing with plaster, charcoal or earth dust will absorb what moisture may remain when nearly dry.　As Carrot seed vegetates somewhat slowly and the plants are quite small when they first appear, weeds are apt to get the start of them before the rows can be seen with sufficient distinctness to make it safe to use the slide hoe.　For this reason many farmers practice soaking the seed in water and keeping it at a temperature that will nearly develop the sprout, before planting.　This may be done by soaking the seed from 36 to 48 hours in milk warm, rather strong manure water, then removing it to where the air is of about the same temperature.　Stir it slightly for a few days, and finally dry it sufficiently to drop freely from the machine by adding plaster, charcoal or dust.　Camphor has a wonderful effect in stimulating the vitality of seed, and the addition of a small quantity of it to the manure water would doubtless be of advantage.　This process should not be carried so far as to develop the sprout.　Should the surface of the ground be very dry when the seed is sown, this soaking process may be fatal, for if the germ is once started it will not live in a dormant state ; it must either grow or die : whereas, seed that have not been soaked will vegetate after rains wet the dry surface.　Be sure that the seed planter has a good roller attached to it, and not a mere coverer, as this will help confine the moisture and thus materially aid in developing the seed.

QUANTITY TO THE ACRE.

Tables vary greatly, some advising as high as four pounds to the acre.　If the design is to raise small-sized roots for early marketing, possibly this might not be an excess of seed, but to advise so heavy seeding for ordinary field crops, means that much of the seed is poor trash, probably old and worthless, and put in as a make-weight.

Some years ago a party wrote me, offering a variety of garden seed at a very low figure, and stated that it was of his own raising.   As it was a kind that I was in the habit of raising, I had the curiosity to write and ask how he could afford to raise it at such a price.   He replied that it was of his own growing, but so old as to be good for nothing, and therefore he sold it to seedsmen at a very low figure, to mix with their good seed to *help make weight!* When four pounds of Carrot seed are advised to the acre, for a field crop, I think that some of this kind of seed must somehow have got into the mixture. With everything favoring, and the farmer by experience having his seed sower under perfect control, rather less than a pound of seed will be sufficient for an acre.   The great object to aim at is, while having the plants thick enough, not to have much of any thinning to do, as it costs about as much to thin a crop as it does to weed it, with the drawback that the plants left in the ground are more or less started, and so put back by the thinning.   As a general rule I would advise one and one-half pounds of seed to the acre, and this the farmer can reduce in proportion as he is favored by circumstances and advances in experience.

Twelve inches is a sufficient distance between the rows of the two small, early varieties, and fifteen between the rows of all other sorts.   With the greatest of care the seed will not come up with mathematical precision.   Some advocate leaving a plant to about every inch of row ; others, to thin to four inches apart.   Carrots are somewhat like Onions in their aptitude to grow to a good size when crowded, pushing out either side of the rows, and at times crops will give great bulk when the plants are nearer each other than four inches; still, as a rule I advise thinning to near this distance, leaving them thicker near vacant places.

VARIETIES, AND WHAT KINDS TO GROW.

Foreign catalogues give lists of about two dozen varieties, which differ in earliness, size, color, form, termination of root, characteristic of growing entirely under or partly above ground, and in the size of the core or heart. In foreign catalogues, what we call "Orange," are known as "Red" Carrots. From a test of these varieties I have thus far found nothing worthy of being added to the kinds already grown to a greater or less extent in the United States. The yellow-fleshed sorts are repudiated in New England by general consent; yet the Yellow Belgian, on a limited trial has proved with me, to be an exceptionably good keeper. The Purple or Blood-Red is of a deep purple color, a poor cropper and by no means attractive to the eye. The remaining varieties may be classed as follows :—Early, middling early and late. The first class is made up of the Early Very Short Scarlet, and the Early Scarlet Horn. The second class, of all the half-long or short horn varieties, and the third, of the long varieties, such as Long Orange, Belgian and Altringham sorts.

In addition to about one-half of these foreign varieties, cultivated more or less generally in this country, there are several kinds catalogued by seedsmen, all of which are but improved strains made by careful selections, through a series of years, from what was originally imported stock. These strains usually bear the name of some person. A brief discussion of the more valuable varieties will now be in order. Here I will lay down three general facts, viz. :—1st, that of the various orange colored varieties, the shorter growing kinds are, as a rule, the darker colored and sweeter flavored. 2d, that the proportion of dark, orange-colored roots in any crop, while it will depend largely on the care that has been used in the selection of seed stock for a series of years, does

not turn wholly on this, but soil, season or manure, one or all
have some influence in this direction.   3d, that the fact that
more or less of the Carrots tend to push seed shoots the first
year, while with the long varieties it may prove that the seed
has been allowed to mix with the wild varieties, yet the prob-
ability, (marked cases excepted,) is decidedly the other
way ; while with the short horn varieties this tendency to
push seed shoots the first season, so as to make something
of a show when an acre is glanced over, is quite a common
characteristic with seed of the very purest strain.

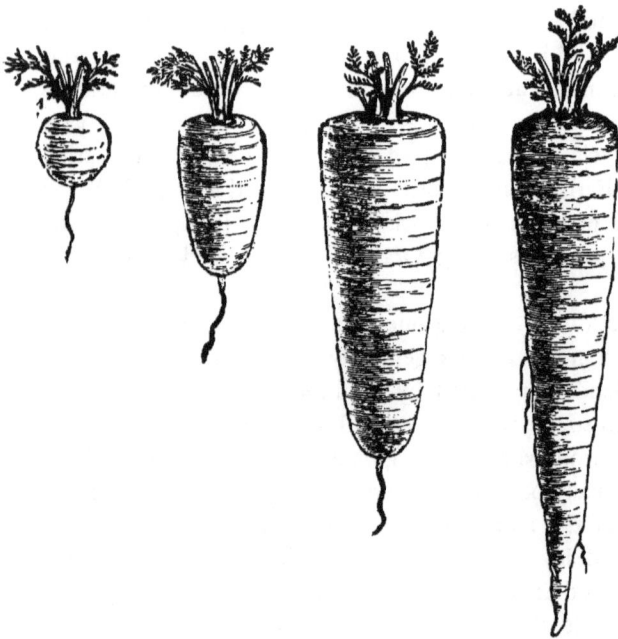

EARLY VERY   EARLY SHORT
SHORT SCARLET.   SCARLET.   SHORT HORN.   LONG ORANGE.

Early Very Short Scarlet. (see engraving.)

Early Short Scarlet Horn. (see engraving.)   These two varieties are the shortest grown and are raised at times in forcing beds, for an early market, the former very generally so.   They are of a very rich orange color, fine-grained, sweet, and of excellent flavor, heading the list for quality. Their rich color makes them valuable above all other kinds for coloring butter.   Though quite short, yet the Early Short Scarlet Horn can be grown to yield a great bulk ol roots, from the fact that from the smallness of their tops the roots can be grown very thick, two or three abreast all along the rows. When the small, handy size of this variety is considered in connection with the superior quality, it stands foremost as a table Carrot, and I therefore recommend it in preference to all others for family use.

Short Horn. (See engraving.)   This variety, intermediate between the Early Forcing and Long Orange, with but slight variations in form, is shown under various names, as Intermediate, Nantes, Half Long, James' Improved, Stump-Rooted, &c.   It is characterized by a darker color than the average of the Long Orange, finer grain, and a sweeter and richer flavor.   In part from the more solid structure of the Carrot, and in part from its better stowage, thirty-six measured bushels of this variety make a ton, while of the larger varieties forty bushels are required.   The best strain of this variety is doubtless the kind known as the "Danvers" Carrot.

Danvers Carrot.   In the town of Danvers, Mass., the raising of Carrots on an extensive scale, has for years been quite a business—the farmers finding a large market in the neighboring cities of Salem, Lynn and Boston.   After years of experimenting they settled upon a variety which originated among them (as did the Danvers Onion) known in their locality as the "Danvers Carrot."   It is in form about

midway between the Long Orange and Short Horn class,
growing very generally with a stump root.   The great problem
in Carrot growing is to get the greatest bulk with the smallest
length of root, and this is what the Danvers growers have
attained in their Carrot.   Under their cultivation they raise
from twenty to forty tons to the acre.   This Carrot is of a
rich, dark orange in color, very smooth and handsome, and
from its length, is easier to dig than the Long Orange.   It is
a first-class Carrot for any soil.

Long Orange, or Long Surry.   This is a standard
variety, and in its various strains is doubtless more generally
grown than any other kind.   The chief objection to it is the
depth to which it penetrates the ground, and hence the extra

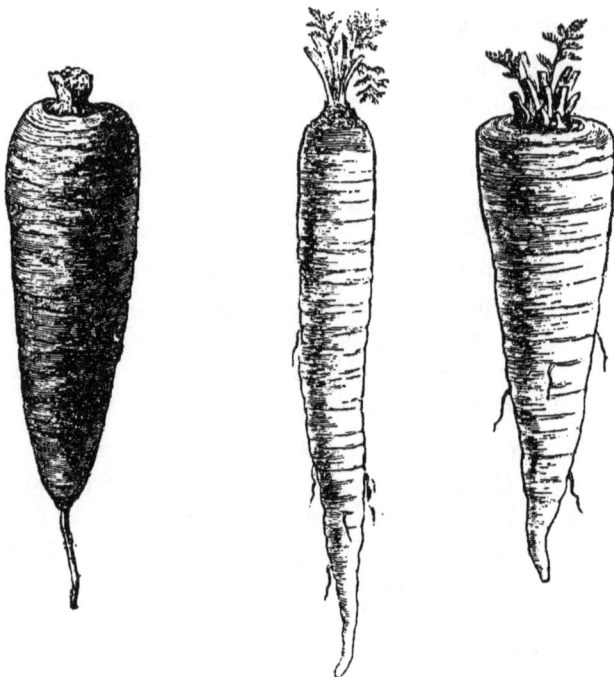

DANVERS CARROT   ALTRINGHAM.   IMPROVED LONG ORANGE.

work of digging it; while the end of the root which causes
the extra work is of inferior quality when compared with
the body, differing in this respect from the shorter varieties,
which are of the same quality
throughout. The heart is larger in
proportion than in the shorter varieties, which is considered an objection. The keeping properties are
excellent, and in this respect it is
superior to the earlier kinds. On
light soil the roots grow long, straight
and make a fine show in the market.

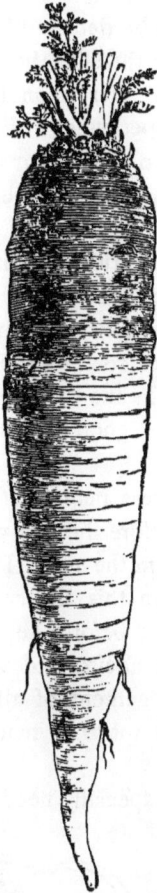

Altringham. This is a Carrot of
excellent quality for the table, the
flesh being of a rich orange color,
crisp and sweet, but as a cropper it
is inferior to the Intermediate or
Long Orange varieties, and hence is
but little cultivated.

Large White Belgian. This is
the largest of all varieties and will
yield at least a quarter more than
any other sort. The roots grow several inches out of ground, and all
can be readily pulled by the hand.
Analysis shows that it is nearly as
sweet as the Mangold Wurtzel, rather
sweeter than the Swede Turnip, and
about two thirds as sweet as the Sugar Beet. The two objections to it

LARGE WHITE BELGIAN. are its color and its keeping properties; it being rather a poor keeper, while the color has
made it a carrot for horses rather than cows. If farmers
have but a small quantity of manure, the White Belgian is
a good variety for them to raise for feeding early in the winter.

THE CULTIVATION, AND THE IMPLEMENTS
NEEDED.

Just as soon as the young plants can be detected breaking ground, the prudent farmer will push the slide hoe, and
have his boy weeders follow immediately after it on hands
and knees. Boys that have had a little experience, with their
nimble fingers can do more work than men, while their wages
are only about half as much. On the sea-coast we hire boys
who make a business of weeding, for from seventy-five cents
to a dollar a day. The one great danger in hiring boys, is that
careless ones are apt to break off the weeds instead of pulling them up by the roots. To ascertain their comparative
faithfulness, it is well to quietly mark a few rows of the different weeders, at their first weeding, and by the time for the
second weeding the difference between a good and a bad
boy will be very plainly visible.

Don't accept that theory of the shiftless man, that it is
well to have the weeds grow pretty tall before the first weeding, that the plants may be protected from the sun. I have
noticed that oftentimes those who act on this theory give
over their weeding, and plough up the bed before they have
half finished it. Promptness in the first hoeing and weeding is exceedingly important in the management of all root
crops, and it is where the great mistake is apt to be made in
their cultivation.

There are a few implements that are specially needed in
the cultiva-
tion of root
crops, and of
these every
wise farmer
will get the

SLIDE HOE.

very best attainable. These implements are the Seed Sower, the Hand Weeder, the Slide Hoe, the common Wheel Hoe, and one for weeding both sides of a row at the same time. Of these there are a great many varieties, each of which are more or less popular among a class of growers. The engravings illustrate such as are in use in my own section of country, where root culture forms a very important part of the agriculture of farmers.   Both the slide and the wheel hoe, for rapid work, far surpass the common hand hoe, while they cut up the weeds equally clear.   The wheel hoe is used until the tops of the crops become so large as to be in the way,

WHEEL HOE

when the slide hoe takes its place. Each should be two inches narrower than the space between the rows.   A slide hoe is an amazing handy implement about a farm for many uses other than between the rows of root crops.   A new class of implements have been introduced within a few years which, to a degree, supersede the use of the common wheel or slide hoe, though there is yet a valuable sphere for each of them ; I refer to the weeders which cut each side of the row at the same time

GOODWIN'S WHEEL HOE.

I have tested every variety of these and have thus far found none do such good, practical work as the homeliest looking one of them all, viz.: the Goodwin wheel hoe.   These hoes which take each side of the row at once cannot safely be made to go over the ground as fast as those designed for use between the rows, but working close home to the growing crop, they save a large portion of the cost of hard weeding. Of seed drills there are a dozen or more in the market, several of which I have used on my farms. I prefer Matthew's over all others. Among other advantages it can be relied upon to

MATTHEW'S SEED SOWER.

drop almost any variety of small seed, while it is a good coverer, and having a roller attached, it packs the earth over

NOYES' WEEDER

the seed, which, as every farmer knows, tends to keep the moisture in and thus hastens their germination. The hand weeder is an excellent little implement to facilitate the laborious work of weeding, especially when the surface is baked and therefore rather hard on the fingers.

GATHERING AND STORING THE CROP.

One of the greatest outlays attending the raising of Carrots is in the gathering and topping of the crop. The common process of digging with a fork and throwing into piles to be afterwards topped is laborious and costly. The labor and consequent cost may be greatly lessened by first cutting off the tops by a sharp shovel, spade or common hoe, or a slide hoe which has been weighted by a piece of lead pipe, or some similar heavy article, slid down the handle and fastened where that unites with the hoe. Should a slice be taken off the tops of the roots it will do no harm, as Carrots differ in this respect from other roots, in that, when the tops are cut they are not apt to rot ; indeed, some practice cutting off a slice of the root when topping, to keep them from sprouting so readily when stored.

Let the crop remain out as late as it can be risked without freezing ; and if they are in good growing condition this will be well towards November, in the latitude of central New England, and even into the first week of that month in the milder temperature of the sea-coast. Roots not fully matured will keep better than those fully ripe when dug, on the principle that the varieties of apples we call "winter" apples are simply those kinds that do not ripen on the tree,—they are not winter apples, because they are Baldwins, or Greenings, for these same kinds in the South where the ripening season is longer, are Fall apples. If the carrots have been planted too early they will ripen before digging and be apt to prove poor keepers, besides losing the advantage of October weather which is the carrot month, doing more for the weight of the late planted crop than all the season besides.

Rake the tops off the bed but do not waste them for they are highly relished by animals, and if the carrots are harvested when they ought to be, to keep well, that is, when in good growing condition, there will be a great weight of tops, sometimes as high as a quarter of the weight of roots ; and this mass of green fodder, coming at a time when the fields are usually bare of grasses, will prove very valuable and acceptable food for the cows. The common way of gathering the crop, by loosening with spades or forks and then pulling out by the tops, throwing into heaps or scattering over the ground and afterwards topping with a knife, is a long and costly job. An improvement on digging is to run a plough close to the row and then pull out as many as possible by hand and dig up the remainder. Still a better course particularly when the Danvers variety is grown, is, beginning in the middle of the piece, to run a subsoil plough close home to the roots, when, if run sufficiently deep it will lift the carrots a little out of the ground. Follow with forks or hoes, and draw the roots inward on the ploughed portion, so far as to give room for the horse to walk. Let the roots remain a few hours scattered over the surface, when in picking up and tossing them into carts or baskets, any earth adhering will be jarred off. In storing, one fact must be borne in mind; that carrots will heat, sprout and rot, under circumstances in which Mangolds would keep sound and uninjured. I have several times lost quantities when buried in the ground where Mangolds and common table Beets, under precisely the same conditions, have kept perfectly sound. If the crop is to be fed at once, they may be dumped into the cellar or barn floor in the most expeditious way without reference to the depth of the heap; but if to be fed into the winter, then all depth of the heap above two and a half to three feet means a proportionate increase of danger of heating, sprouting and rotting, and so much greater care to air the cellar in cool, dry weather. I need hardly state that cellars for keeping carrots and all roots should be free from standing water, and as cool as possible without actually freezing. If the bottom is damp, then put down a rough flooring. When the roots are large they will keep sufficiently better to pay for the extra trouble, if they are piled "heads and points" to the height of two and a half feet, with a slight space for air between the piles. If there are not cellar conveniences for storing the entire crop, with a good protection of hay under and around them, a few tons may be stored, for early feeding, in the barn, provided it is a warm one.

RAISING CARROTS WITH ONIONS.

I transfer from my Treatise on Onions, a paragraph relative to growing carrots with onions.

The plan of raising carrots with onions is considered a great improvement by many who have adopted it, as the yield of carrots is thought to be clear gain, diminishing but little or none the yield of onions. Carrots are planted in two ways; one by sowing them in drills between every other row of onions, and the other, which is considered an improvement, called the Long Island plan, by planting the onions in hills from seven to eight inches from center to center, dropping a number of seed in each hill, and from the first to the twelfth of June planting the carrot seed, usually by hand, between these hills in two rows, then skipping one, and thus on through the piece. The onions, as they are pulled are thrown into every third row, the carrots being left to mature. By this method from two to six hundred bushels of carrots are raised per acre in addition to the usual crop of onions. More manure is required for the two crops than for the onions alone.

The machine used for sowing in drills has two boxes attached to the axle at equi-distance from the wheels; there are three or four holes in the axle that communicate with the seed in the boxes, and as these holes pass under the boxes they are filled with seed, and as they turn the seed are dropped into the earth. Screws are sunk into the holes, which can be sunk more or less at pleasure, and the quantity of seed which the holes will contain is thus graded.

The machine should first be tested and so regulated that on a barn floor it will drop from eleven to twelve seed from each hole. When so regulated, on using in the field it will drop but from seven to twelve, owiwg to the more uneven motion.

MARKETING AND FEEDING.

In the cities there is a large market for carrots as feed for horses, it being very generally accepted that a few given daily or every other day, aids the digestion of grain-fed animals, adds to the gloss of the hair, and are of special medicinal value. The largest, smoothest and darkest orange colored roots sell the best in the market. The price varies all the way from ten to twenty dollars a ton of 2000 pounds, depending in part on the value of hay. Where the quantity fed daily is small a large knife or a shovel will answer to cut them up in pieces of suitable size ; but if the quantity amounts to several bushels daily, then a root-cutter will be needed. There are two classes of these, one for sheep, and the other for large stock, the essential difference being that those designed to cut roots for sheep cut into smaller pieces. Of those designed to cut roots for large stock, the Whittemore machine is as good a machine as any, having a capacity to cut up a bushel in about half a minute. Among farmers there is much unnecessary fear about the danger of animals choking while feeding on apples, potatoes and roots. For the last ten years I have fed to my cows not far from three hundred tons of squashes, potatoes and roots, (mostly squashes) and never yet lost an animal or had any very serious trouble from choking. My habit is to feed them while quietly in their stalls, with a division board between the feed of each. All cases of choking that have come to my notice have occurred *where the animal was suddenly disturbed while eating.* There is a great difference of opinion as to how many roots can be fed to stock daily without injuring them. The proportion will depend somewhat on the constitutional peculiarities of individual cows, but when the bowels are all right the appetite of the animal is probably the safest guide. I have had a large and extended experience in feed-

ing squashes to milch cows,—the Boston Marrow, Hubbard
and other varieties ; beginning with half a bushel to each
animal, I increase the quantity until the daily consumption
has averaged a hundred pounds a day to each.   Under
such heavy feeding, after a while their appetites clog somewhat, but I am inclined to the opinion that, beginning with a
moderate feed, they would soon readily eat seventy-five
pounds daily with a relish, for as long a period as they might
last.   When feeding Carrots or any roots, the most economical method is to give meadow or salt hay, with a small quantity of flax-seed or cotton-seed meal.   The effect of the roots
and these rich meals is to give to these inferior varieties
of hay, the nutritious value of the best upland English.

MANGOLD WURTZELS.

What is a Mangold Wurtzel? A number of years ago I raised a piece of Early Turnip Beet seed in a very isolated location ; there was not another piece of Beet seed growing t within half a mile, at the least. A good deal of the seed wasted, as is usual when the seed is allowed to ripen well on the stock before cutting. From this waste seed thousands of young plants sprang up, many of which survived the winter, by the help of the protection of chickweed and snow. They had got so far along when ploughing time came, I left the piece unploughed, thinning them out that they might produce early beets. As the season advanced a good many of them pushed seed shoots and ripened a crop of seed. Some of the seed I gathered and the next season planted it to see what it would produce. The crop was "everything ;" all the way from a nice, dark colored Early Turnip Beet, through different sizes, colors and forms, up to a light-fleshed Mangold Wurtzel. As the original Beets were a very pure Turnip Beet, and during several years of careful cultivation for seed purposes had shown no admixture with any other variety, the experiment proved either that the coarse variety of Stock Beet, which we call Mangold Wurtzel are but sports from our fine-grained table Beets, or that the Beet class are sports from Mangolds,—most probably the former.

Mangold Wurtzels differ from table Beets in their general coarseness of structure, and the larger size to which they grow, the elements which enter into the composition of each being the same in kind. I have grown an ordinary Turnip Beet to weigh twenty-three pounds, and of the size of a half bushel measure. At times, on rich, friable soil, the Long Blood Beet will attain to large proportions, but when led by such results to attempt to get equal weight with Mangolds, under first-rate conditions, the experiment, with me, has uniformly failed. Still, when quality is wanted, in the fattening of hogs for instance, I am not certain but that the food obtained from an acre of the large variety of table Beets, may not be more than that obtained from an equal acre in Mangolds.

What is a Sugar Beet? The term "Sugar Beet" is an unfortunate one, as the word "Sugar" had already been appropriated to express the sweet flavor of the varieties of Beets raised for table use, while the word Beet is strictly a misnomer, the vegetable Sugar Beet being in reality a Mangold Wurtzel. A generation ago our fathers used the term "Sugar" as a familiar designation for any sweet variety of beet raised for table use, and at the present by the great majority of the public the term is still so used. As the new industry of manufacturing sugar from the beet grew on the continent of Europe, seedsmen were called upon to supply for commerce seed of the best variety for this purpose. It was necessary that this variety should be as free as possible from all coloring substance as this would, as a matter of course, give a stain to the juice, and impose on the manufacturer the labor of purifying it. The ones at first selected were the long, white Mangold Wurtzels, and these were called the "Sugar" Beet in commercial parlance. These white Mangolds were not entirely white, the portion that grew above ground being usually colored a light green by exposure to the sun's rays; it became therefore an object for the manufacturer to still improve on them to the end that all the coloring should be eliminated. The intelligence and enterprise of the seedsmen of Europe responded to this want, and in the course of a few years two prominent varieties were produced, that have nearly completely satisfied it,—one of these was sent out by the estimable house of Vilmorin Andrieux & Co., of Paris, and is named "Vilmorin's New Improved White," and the other "White Imperial Extra," by the distinguished German house of Ernest Benary.

These improved Sugar Beets of commerce grow nearly entirely under ground, and when grown these beets define themselves to be the Mangold variety, by the coarser structure of the root, the stouter ribs and the greater coarseness of the leaves, which spring in larger masses directly from the crown, than is the case with beets for the table.

The moral of all this for my farmer friends is, that if you want a beet for table use do not order "Sugar Beet" or you will be very likely to find a Mangold growing in your garden, a return, but not a recompense for the sweat and toil of the husbandman.

VARIETIES.

About twenty varieties are catalogued by seedsmen, many of which are but strains of the same kind, bearing the name of the grower, who by careful cultivation has endeavored to improve it. Classified by form they come under three classes, viz. :—the long, the round and the ovoid or intermediate varieties. Classified by color we have the red or scarlet, the pink, the yellow or orange, and the white varieties.

The Long Varieties.—Among the more prominent of these are the Ox Horn, the common Long Red, Sutton's

Imperial, Norbiton Giant, Long Egyptian, Carter's Improved, the Long Yellow, and the Silesian varieties of Sugar Beet. The Ox Horn is a very crooked growing variety, as its name would imply, with a small diameter in proportion to its great length. Growing almost wholly out of ground it curves about so in the row as to be decidedly in the way, is apt to break when pulled and in addition to these defects, storing very badly, it is not in any way desirable. The Norbiton Giant, Carter's Mammoth Long Red, Sutton's Imperial, and Long Elvethan are improvements over the common Long Red in a greater uniformity in their habit of growth, their size, and a less liability to grow hollow at the top at the advanced stage of growth.

The Round Varieties.—In these are included the common Red and Yellow Globe, with some of the under-ground varieties of the Sugar Beet.

Ovoid are either red or yellow in color and are intermediate in form between the long and the round kinds.

LONG RED.MANGOLD.

What Kinds to Grow.—In this country the Long Red are the most popular, particularly the Norbiton Giant

variety. While
travelling in Eng-
land, Ireland and
France, for inquiry
and observation, I
found that the
round and ovoid
varieties were more
generally cultivat-
ed than the long
sorts. In my ex-
perience the ovoid
varieties incline
to grow smooth-
er than the long
kinds and hence
are likely to bring
up less earth with
them, which on
heavy soil is a
matter of some

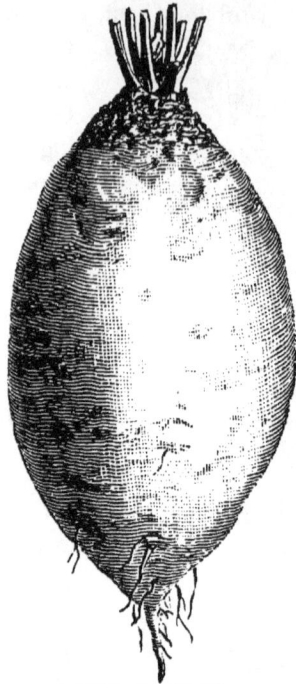

OVOID MANGOLD.

moment. I think of the two kinds the yellow, under the
same circumstances, makes the larger root. The long varieties pile better in the cellar, while the round or ovoids cut
up rather more readily, appear less inclined to rot at the top,
and are firmer fleshed. The globe and ovoid varieties appear to be best adapted to hard and shallow soils, and of
these the Yellow Globe and Ovoid are especially valuable,
as they are better keepers than most sorts and remain sound,
without sprouting, until late into the spring, and with special
care may be kept even into the summer season.

The long Silesian varieties of Sugar Beet vary from
each other only in the color of the part exposed above
ground,—being green, grey or red. The kind intro-

duced to the American public a few years ago, under the name of Lane's Improved American Sugar Beet, is a strain of the Long White Mangold. The improved varieties of Germany and France yield about double the per centage of sugar that is found in the common Mangold, in some crops the proportion being as high as thirteen per cent. This would make the Sugar Beets of double the value of Mangolds for stock, but unfortunately, the roots under like conditions of cultivation, average but half the weight of Mangolds.

As this treatise is about roots as food for stock, the cultivation of beet for the manufacture of sugar is not

GLOBE MANGOLD.

within its sphere, yet I must express surprise that with the experience of Germany and France to draw from and our own inventive skill and enterprise to add to it, we have not as yet made marked advance in this department of manufacturing industry. The average percentage of sugar found in analysis of beets grown in this country is exceptionably high. Land free from alkalies, of unbounded fertility, readily accessible, being attainable at almost nominal cost, it is a standing puzzle why we do not follow the example of other countries and raise our own sugar rather than import it. Perhaps the conundrum will be solved yet by some associate enterprise among our farmers, similar to that which gave birth to our cheese factory system; the inducement in this case being the home market that the sugar factory would afford for unlimited areas of beets, while the refuse pulp would enable them to increase greatly the number of their neat stock, to the advantage of the manure pile and enlargement of their area of tillage.

THE SOIL AND ITS PREPARATION.

In the matter of soil, Mangold Wurtzels will accept a greater latitude than any other root; thriving on every variety, all the way from light loam to muck, and from that to as strong a clay as is sufficiently friable for tillage. Muck (properly drained) and a strong loam are best suited to develop pounds of crop. Though the crop grown in the lighter soil is not so great, it is much sweeter than when grown on heavy soil, and when extraordinary quantities of manure have been applied, some of the heaviest crops on record have been grown on light loam. The great crop of Mr. Fearing of Hingham, of over sixty tons to the acre, was raised on a sandy loam. Some years ago I took a purchaser into the field where two lots of Mangolds were growing; he selected at once the large roots on the low land. I asked him to taste a slice of those on the upland, when he at once changed his preference. As a rule it will be found that those grown on warm, upland soil are decidedly the sweeter and this fact has an important bearing on the feeding value of the crop.

If the soil is in good heart for a foot in depth, plough it to that depth before putting on the manure. After putting on the manure, if coarse, it will be well to cut it up with Randall's wheel-harrow before ploughing under. After cross ploughing the manure four or five inches beneath the surface the aim should be to make a good seed bed by getting the surface level and the soil light and fine. On most soils this can be accomplished by a liberal use of the wheel-harrow followed by a fine-toothed smoothing harrow and that by a plank drag. An old barn door will sometimes answer for this, but as it is an excellent implement on the farm it will be well to have one. It should be about three feet wide and six long, with one side about ten inches high, meeting the bottom at an angle of forty-five degrees; the planks had better overlap slightly, as they will the better break the lumps of earth. The team is to be hitched to the turned up side, and the driver is to stand on the drag, driving it sideways over the land. The effect of such a drag in breaking up lumps and generally pulverizing the soil, will be found to be much superior to that of any roller. Should the soil be of such a character or in such a condition that the harrow and drag process will not make a good seed bed, there remains no resource other than to prepare it as for onions, by raking over the entire surface.

THE MANURE AND ITS APPLICATION.

The kind and quantities of food needed to grow any vegetable is found by an analysis of that vegetable. Having thus learned the kind and quantity needed for any crop, the next step of the wise farmer will be to ascertain what manures contain the necessary constituents and which of these contain them in the cheapest form. A little knowledge of Chemistry, in its application to manures, is of incalculable value to the husbandman and no amount of experience and traditionary knowledge can serve as a substitute for it. I believe that it is in this direction that the great advance in agriculture will be made, and were there no other argument for Agricultural colleges the fact that they are prepared to give thorough instruction in this one department would be a sufficient reason for their existence, and for their liberal patron-

age by their several states. Prof. Voelcker, an excellent au
thority in everything that pertains to chemistry, in its appli
cation to agriculture, gives the following table as the average
composition of the ash of the principal root crops.

AVERAGE COMPOSITION OF THE ASH OF ROOTS.									
	Number of Analyses.	Potash.	Soda.	Lime.	Magnesia.	Oxide of Iron.	Phosphoric Acid.	Sulphuric Acid.	Silica.	Chlorine.
TURNIPS.	38	49.8	7.8	11.7	2.6	0.9	10.3	11.8	1.2	5.0
SWEDES.	7	38.9	14.0	12.8	4.2	0.8	10.4	13.7	1.9	4.2
MANGOLDS.	12	46.6	18.4	5.9	4.8	0.8	8.3	3.7	4.0	9.9
SUGAR BEET.	40	48.0	10.4	6.4	9.5	1.0	14.4	4.7	3.8	2.3
CARROTS.	10	37.0	20.7	10.9	5.2	1.0	11.2	6.9	2.0	4.9
PARSNIPS.	4	46.7	2.7	15.7	6.0	1.3	15.8	5.6	2.4	4.0

LEAF ASH.									
TURNIPS.	37	27.6	5.1	33.2	2.6	2.0	7.3	13.1	3.5	7.7
SWEDES.	3	21.9	12.3	30.2	3.2	2.0	6.4	10.6	4.8	11.0
MANGOLDS.	4	25.5	23.3	10.4	9.7	1.2	5.4	7.2	3.3	17.8
SUGAR BEET.	7	21.9	16.6	19.5	18.1	1.3	7.3	7.9	3.1	5.7
CARROTS.	7	17.6	18.2	32.1	3.9	3.0	3.8	8.2	5.2	8.9

This table shows us that the Mangolds require the mineral ingredients of manure in the following order, when arranged with reference to their importance :—Potash, Soda,
Chlorine, Lime, Phosphoric Acid, Magnesia, Sulphuric Acid,
Silica. In addition to these minerals other substances enter
into the composition of Mangolds, the most important of
which is Nitrogen. Barn-yard manure contains about all the
elements needed by vegetation, but not always in the right
proportion, therefore, when applying it, it is always profitable to know the proportions of the minerals which enter into
crops that the deficiency may be supplied from other sources.
It is perhaps hardly necessary to say that unleached wood

ashes and the German Potash Salts, Sulphate and Muriate, are the cheapest sources for Potash at present known, while Soda and Chlorine are most cheaply obtained from the waste salt of the fisheries. Of this I shall have more to say presently when treating of salt as an auxiliary fertilizer. Lime is most cheaply obtained from the common Carbonate of Lime of the mason, either water or air slacked, and this usually contains more or less of Magnesia. The great source of Phosphoric Acid is the bones of animals or coprolites, by which is meant the fossilized bones and dung of extinct animals; Sulphuric Acid is most cheaply obtained from Plaster, which is Sulphate of Lime.

Some hold great benefit is derived by the crop of the following year, from ploughing under the leaves as soon as the roots are topped; the value of this is just what the analyses of our table shows. The large crops reported as raised in this country, have been raised on soil ranging from light to a friable clay loam and have received all the way from eight to fifteen cords of barn-yard manure to the acre. In some instances this has been all ploughed in; in others half spread broadcast and ploughed in and the other half put in the furrows. When coarse and unfermented I would advise a deep ploughing of it under, in the Fall As with Carrots, other waste substances can be used as substitutes for barn-yard manure, care being taken, either that such waste substances are specially rich in Potash, Soda and Chlorine, or that these substances be added. The equivalents given are roughly estimated under the article treating of the manure for Carrots and will be sufficient for practical purposes; I therefore make no further allusions to these cheap wastes as sources for manure, further than to mention that sea manures are specially rich in potash and soda.

Of all roots Mangolds are the rankest feeders, removing more plant food from the soil than any other root crop. The crop of Mr. Albert Fearing, of Hingham, Mass., was sixty tons of roots, and if the tops were in the usual proportion, of about one-third, they weighed twenty tons more, giving the enormous yield of eighty tons of green food from one acre of ground. The crop raised on Deer Island, in Boston harbor, was about seventy tons to the acre; with a like proportion of tops the total yield must have been over a hundred tons. In the sewage farms of England eighty tons of roots have been raised on an acre of ground. Fearing applied fifteen cords of manure to his acre of ground; of the quantity applied to the Deer Island crop I regret I have not the data at hand.

If the mere bulk alone was to be aimed at in the crop, the problem would be a very simple one, but there are three points to be considered: first, how to get a crop that shall be great in bulk and at the same time give us the second desirable point, viz.: *ripeness*, and thus insure the third desirable point, viz.: *the highest percentage of sugar it is possible for the roots to acquire.*

This matter of the value of Mangolds, for feeding purposes, being in about the same proportion as the sugar present, though appertaining to that part of this Treatise which treats of "Feeding to Stock," yet has so direct a bearing on the manuring of the crops that I will take it up at this place. The recent researches of that distinguished chemist, Prof. Voelcker of England, than whom there is no better authority, has thrown much light on the question of manure in its application to this crop. The Professor takes the position that the nutritious value of roots is in proportion to the amount of dry matter in them, and that the percentage of sugar present coincides with that of dry matter, the proportion of sugar rising or falling with the percentage of dry matter in the roots. That the feeding value does not depend on the proportion of nitrogen they contain, is proved theoretically, by the fact that the percentage is very much higher in the early stages of growth, before the crop is matured, than it is later in the season, while in the experiments of Mr. Lawes in feeding sheep, the lot containing the most nitrogen in the way of nutrition gave the poorest results.

Assuming with Prof. Voelcker that bulk should not be sought at a disproportionate sacrifice of sugar in the crop, and that certain soils and certain manures and certain methods of cultivation are more favorable than others to the development of this desirable proportion. I present extracts from his valuable article on "Root Crops as affected by Soil and Manures."

"Land highly manured with rich dung from the fattening boxes or stables, induces luxurious and vigorous growth in root crops, and, as is well known, has a tendency to develop over-luxuriance in the tops. This is the case more particularly if the dung is derived from fattening beasts, liberally supplied with oil-cake and artificial food, rich in nitrogenous constituents. If the Autumn turns out fairly dry and warm, the roots in highly manured land continue to grow vigorously, the bulbs swell to a large dimension, and if the weather in September and October continues warm and dry, a heavy weight, and fairly ripe roots, result from the liberal use of rich dung. But should the Autumn be cold and wet, too liberal an application of good, well-rotten dung is apt to maintain the luxuriant tops in a vigorous, active-growing condition, at a period of the year when the crop has to be taken up, and the result is an immature root crop, of a low feeding value. Although the bulbs may be of a good size, they turn out, when grown under such conditions, watery, deficient in sugar, and not nearly as nutritious as they would have been had a more moderate dressing of dung been put upon the land. The main cause of the immature condition and low-feeding quality of Mangolds grown with an excess-

ive quantity of rich dung is the comparatively large amount
of ammonial and nitrogenous constituents in the dung; for
numerous field experiments have shown that the peculiar tendency of ammonia salts, and of readily available nitrogenous
substances is to induce luxuriant leaf-development and vigorous and prolonged growth, which results frequently in a
more or less immature condition of the roots.   There is thus
danger of over-manuring crops; and the desire to produce
heavy crops of Mangolds not unfrequently leads practical
men not to appreciate sufficiently this danger.   It is quite
true Mangolds are very greedy feeders, and no doubt some
soils will swallow up almost any amount of dung; but at the
same time it has to be borne in mind that all land is not
alike, and that there are many naturally rich clay loams containing immense stores of plant food, which requires only to
be brought into play by good cultivation in order to become
available to plants.   I am much inclined to think that it is a
mistake to manure soils of the latter description too liberally
with dung, even for Mangolds, and that in many cases a
more economical result, and certainly a better quality of
Mangolds, although not so heavy a crop, would be given, if,
instead of all the enormous dressings of dung which are
often applied to that crop, the land were manured in Autumn
with only half the quantity of dung, and the seed drilled in
with three to four cwt. of superphosphate or dissolved bones,
which manures, as we shall see presently have a tendency to
produce early maturity in roots.   We frequently hear of
complaints that Mangolds scour, or do not keep well.   Complaints of this kind are only the expressions in other words
for the immature condition of the roots, and in many cases
the cause of this undesirable condition has to be sought in
the excessive amount of ammonial or nitrogenous constituents which are applied to the Mangolds in the shape of
heavy dressings of dung.   The same remarks apply with

equal force to the exclusive and too abundant use of Peru
vian guano, sulphate of ammonia and nitrogenous manures
in general. The special effect of all ammonial and nitrogenous manures in general, as already stated, is to produce luxuriant leaf development, to induce prolonged and vigorous
growth, resulting in an immature and watery condition of the
bulbs.

Large roots, generally speaking, are far less nutritious
than better matured roots of a moderate size. For illustration of this fact I quote the following comparative analyses :

	Water.	Nitrogenous Constituents	Sugar, Pectine, &c.	Crude Fibre.	Ash.
MANGOLDS 9 lbs.	91.85	1.34	2.86	2.54	1.41
" 7 1-2 lbs.	89.48	1.24	3.95	4.51	.82
" 4 lbs.	89.77	0.73	7.68	.89	.93
" 1 to 2 lbs.	86.90	0.61	10.51	1.07	.91

Small Mangolds approach Sugar Beets in composition,
whilst large Sugar Beets are hardly better than common
Mangolds, and monster beets are even less nutritious than
well-matured Mangolds of fair average size. Monster roots,
as is well known, are always very watery, poor in sugar, and
almost useless for feeding purposes.

Big Berkshire beets,—one weighing 16 pounds and the
other 12 1-4 pounds,—contained only 3.89 or 4 per cent. of
sugar respectively, and in round numbers as much as 91 1-2
per cent. of water. This high percentage of water is ac-
companied by a larger amount of albuminous compounds
and of mineral matter, than the proportions in roots, containing very much more solid feeding matter- A large amount
of albuminous matter and of ash, indeed indicates immatur-
ity and poverty in sugar, a characteristic of big, excessively
manured roots.

"Generally speaking, all nitrogenous manure, either should not be used at all, or only sparingly, for roots, on stiffish land, and all soils which contain a good deal of clay, are naturally cold and unfavorable to a vigorous and rapid growth. On the other hand, raw, or better still, dissolved Peruvian guano is an excellent manure for root crops upon light land, which, like most productive sandy soils and friable turnip loams, favors the quick and vigorous growth of roots, and is condu;ive to early maturity.

"Nitrate of soda has the same general effect upon root crops as nitrogenous manures, but it appears to be more energetic in its action, and, on the whole, to be a useful addition to home manures, and to increase the produce in roots more considerably than salts of ammonia. Its effect is specially marked upon mangolds, and, to my knowledge, heavy crops of mangolds have been produced upon rather light land by 1 1-2 per cent. of Nitrate of Soda, two cwt. of common salt, sown broadcast, and four cwt. of dissolved bones drilled in with the seed.

"Potash salts in some field experiments which I have tried in different parts of the country, have shown that Potash has a decidedly beneficial effect upon root crops, on poor, sandy soils; while on the majority of land, and notably upon clays or clay loams, or soils in a good agricultural condition, Salts of Potash do not increase the produce. The special effect of superphosphates, dissolved bones and similar phosphatic manures, is to produce early maturity; and hence phosphatic manures are employed in practice very largely, and with much benefit, by root growers. In free-growing, light soils, it is desirable either to use dissolved bones in addition to half dressing of farm-yard manure, as a manure for roots, or to spread broadcast 2 or 3 cwt. of salt, or 2 cwt. of guano and 1 cwt. of nitrate of soda and 2 cwt. of common salt, and to drill with the seed 3 to 4 cwt. of dis-

solved bones. On the heavier description of soils it is pref-
erable to use mineral superphosphate for roots, especially if
the land has been dressed in Autumn with a moderate quantity of dung."

SALT AS AN AUXILIARY MANURE.

It will be seen by the table of analysis of roots, that the
Mangold has in it a remarkably large percentage of Chlorine
and Soda, the roots yielding respectively 9.9 and 18.4, while
the tops give, 17.8 and 23.3. Salt being a combination of
Chlorine and Soda, known to chemists as Chloride of Sodium, must therefore be a valuable auxiliary manure for Mangolds, that is, one to be used in connection with other manures. Practice proves what chemistry indicates. Prof·
Voelcker tells us that "salt tends to check over-luxuriance in
the tops, while it prolongs the period of active growth. In
consequence of this specific action it may be employed with
benefit as an auxiliary manure upon light land, in quantities
not greater than five bushels to the acre." Mr. Lewis, of
New York, believes that by scattering over the surface, when
the Mangolds develop the fourth leaf, four or five bushels of
the refuse of the Syracuse salt works, which is about equal
parts of salt and plaster, he has increased his crop ten tons
to the acre. Mr. Lewis finds that salt tends to prevent a dis·
ease which sometimes attacks the leaves, known as "rust.
He states that it can be obtained at the works for about $3.50
per ton. Prof. Voelcker believes it would be injurious rather
than beneficial on heavy land.

The quantity to be applied to the acre as given by practical growers, varies from four to twenty-five bushels. The
effect is not always the same ; one season the increase may
be very striking and the next, under the same application,
not be perceptible, the cause of which is not very clear,

though it appears to give better results in dry seasons than in wet. The most striking effect from the application of large quantities, in my experience, has been on the borders of meadow land. A number of years ago I manured in the furrow with refuse herring bait, salt and all, just as taken from the fish barrels. The crop of Mangolds grown from this manuring was one of the largest and smoothest I ever raised. The next season the land was planted to Oats. In the Fall, while laying a heap of this oat straw in the barn, I chanced to use one as a tooth-pick. It tasted as though it had been pickled ; thinking it was the result of some accident, I took another ; that also was salt. This aroused my curiosity and on examination I found farther, to my great surprise, that all the straw tasted as though it had been dipped in pretty strong brine. Certainly this tremendous salting, over and above what the crop of Mangolds could use, to all appearance, had not lessened the bulk of roots. On meadow land, Mr. Ware of this town, thinks that in a dry season he doubled his crop by the application of refuse salt, at the rate of twenty-five bushels to the acre. In purchasing waste salt for this or any other agricultural crop, it is best to get the dirtiest lot possible, for this dirt is the waste of the fish on which it has been used, and consists mostly of fish scales, which for manuring purposes is decidedly the most valuable part of the fish. For this reason the waste from salted herring is probably the most valuable of all. Under the open platforms where fish are dried, in sea-port towns, and from which there is always some dripping, the rankest of grass grows.   Salt lessens the proportion of sugar in the roots.

PLANTING THE SEED AND TENDING THE CROP.

Our ground being now ready the next step is to plant it. How much seed shall we need and how far apart shall we have the rows? From four to six pounds of seed is the usual quantity, the higher figures evidently allowing for a considerable waste, while with hand planting even the smaller amount may be decreased. As to the proper distance between the rows, practical growers will give various replies ;—18, 20, 22, 24, 30 inches. The thirty inch men are those who expect to depend on the cultivator to do about all their weeding, and are willing to prepare and spare more ground, with the object of having less weeding. That the crop does not require so much room to yield the greatest bulk, is shown by the experience of other cultivators, who have raised from forty to over sixty tons to the acre, with their rows from eighteen to twenty-two inches apart, while the greatest crop on record, viz. :—of over eighty tons to the acre, was raised with the rows twenty-four inches apart.

Planting on ridges is often advised, but as far as I have observed, those who begin this way generally change to the system of level culture as they advance in experience. The only advantages I have found in the system of ridge cultivation have been that the Mangolds appear to grow with fewer roots, and are rather more easily weeded. These advantages in practice are more than off-set by the extra labor of making the ridges and preparing them for planting. Mangold seed is apt to come up badly. In France, where land is cut up into small areas and labor is cheap, one would expect to find as little waste as possible, but while traveling there I noted in their fields that the Mangolds were quite scattering. Mangold seed, like those of beets, are enclosed in a porous shell which itself is usually called the seed. By cracking these "seeds" the real seed will be found within, at the angles, from one to four in number, and when broken, if fresh, appear as white as flour. One reason why a portion of the seed fails to vegetate, is, I infer, from the quantity of moisture necessary to reach and swell the encased seed. For this reason, if planted during dry spells, care should be taken to get them down to a good depth, say an inch and a half deep, and then to pack the fine earth closely over them so that it may hold the moisture. Any machine, therefore, that is used for planting should have a good roller. To facilitate and hasten the vegetation, some cultivators practice soaking the seed, by pouring on water when almost at a scalding temperature, and letting the seed remain in it from thirty-six to forty-eight hours, being careful to keep it where the water will not fall below blood heat, then rolling plaster or dry soil, until it is sufficiently dry to drop readily from the machine.

Some prefer to plant by hand, believing that the greater certainty of getting the seed up and the greater regularity of the plants in the row is more than an off-set to the additional labor. In doing this some growers will drop the seed on the surface by the machine, and then follow and push them under to the depth requisite, with the thumb and finger; others use a strip of plank about four inches wide and three feet in length, on the under side of which are inserted wooden pins, every seven inches, the pins being one and a quarter inches in diameter and projecting two inches. The holes having been made, the seed are dropped in, and covered by the hand. In my own experience I rely on Mathew's seed drill, and find but few blank places after the plants are up, provided the weather is not too dry. Where blanks are found they may be profitably filled by transplanting the young Mangolds, care being taken to break off the tops of the larger leaves, and also to loosen the ground a little when planting them. If a time just after a shower is selected, the result will be very satisfactory. The transplanted roots when gathered in the Fall will usually be found with several small roots in place of a single tap root.

All root crops require prompt and thorough attention in the matter of weeding, and to lessen this costly department of labor they should not be raised on land abounding in the seed of weeds.   Mangolds will require two or three hand weedings, besides as many slidings with the scuffle or wheel-hoe.   If too thick they should be thinned rather early in their growth, for I have oftentimes noticed that if this is left until the roots begin to develop, those left standing are apt to be dwarfed.   It is best to give two thinnings.   The plants should be left from ten to twelve inches apart; the crop of eighty tons was thinned to twelve inches apart, and as the roots are more apt to grow coarse and prongy, and with less sugar in them, when far apart, I am inclined to ten or twelve inches as far enough.   The object aimed at should be, as Prof. Voelcker has shown, to get the weight in many roots of medium size rather than in fewer roots of large size.

GATHERING AND STORING THE CROP.

Unlike other roots, the keeping qualities of Mangolds are destroyed by a temperature low enough to but little more than freeze the surface of the ground.   In the late Fall when the growth is about completed, these much exposed roots have but few leaves to protect them and hence, where freezing weather is feared, the provident farmer will always give them the benefit of the doubt.   If he is so unfortunate as to have his crop injured, let him at once get the most he can out of them, in the way of food, for though the injury at first may appear to be but trivial, the part frozen will become first corky and afterwards turn black, and ultimately rot.   If but slightly frozen the frost may be taken out by at once cover-ing the roots temporarily with earth, but such roots must be fed early or they will rot.   Where the globe or ovoid varie-ties are grown, on land where they pull hard they may be lifted by running a subsoil plough with care.   In pulling these, or any roots that are to be topped on the field, don't do, as is usually done, either scatter them on the surface, without any system, or throw them into heaps, as in either way the cost of removing the tops is increased.   If thrown in piles the tops become more or less intermingled, and the small amount of extra labor thereby caused in topping each individual root becomes great in the aggregate, when thousands are handled.   Still it oftentimes happens that the weather takes a sudden, unexpected turn, threatening too low a temperature for the safety of the crop ; under such circumstances the question is how to get it out of danger in the most expeditious way possible.   The quickest way is to pull and throw into heaps, *roots in*, *tops out*, by which arrangement, should there be considerable of a freeze up, the tops would shield the roots.   To protect them still more effectually earth may be shovelled over the heaps, so as barely to cover them, and when protected in this way they may be allowed to remain quite awhile awaiting the leisure of the farmer.   Here let me say that this plan of protection will not answer for all crops, as I have learnt with Cabbages, to my sorrow, for when covered up this way, but for a few days, when taken out they will be found to be almost cooked by the great heat which they have developed.

In gathering all roots the great object is to have as few handlings as possible, hence, if the tops are not twisted off as the Mangolds are pulled, they should be laid in rows, tops in and roots out, four or more rows being put in one.   It will be best to have two hands work together, and so make two of these rows, leaving a small passage-way between them, the roots being on the inside.   Now let the topper follow with a large and sharp knife, and lop off the leaves to his right and left as he goes being careful to so top the roots that each individual leaf will fall separately, which means that he is not to cut the top of the root itself, for unlike Carrots, Mangolds so cut are apt to decay when stored.   For economical work the knife should be a large and somewhat heavy one, the blade eight or nine inches in length. A small grit stone for the use of each of the hands engaged in topping any kind of roots is always a good investment ; it saves running to the barn for an occasional touch on the grindstone.

If the roots are to be marketed they will need to be left awhile to have the earth on them dry, that it may fall off when loading, but if for use on the farm it will be rather of an advantage, as it will help keep them from wilting. The portion of the crop to be fed before Spring should be stored as near to the place of feeding as possible. The great object should be to keep them sufficiently covered and cool to prevent wilting. As all the beet family are good keepers, there need be but a small per cent. of loss. Store them in a cool, rather moist cellar, provided it has no standing water. The heap may be three or four feet in depth, and should be covered with earth that is rather moist than otherwise, to prevent evaporation. The long varieties may be piled cordwood fashion. Those to be fed after Spring opens can be kept in a pit, dug in gravelly soil, on a hill-side, or where there is no danger from standing water ; the pit may be three or four feet in depth, and be filled to the surface. In covering there are two methods : one, to throw the earth directly on the roots, and the other to first cover them with cornstalks, or some dry, coarse litter before throwing on the earth. In practice I find that when the litter is used the roots in immediate contact with it are apt to mould, more or less, and be affected with a dry rot, though it is an excellent plan to throw over coarse litter up to severe freezing weather. Which ever course is pursued it is best not to throw on more at first than is sufficient to barely cover them, and to add the remainder, making a covering of about two feet in depth in all ; to which is to be added a foot of coarse hay as the weather becomes cold. The process of

thatching with straw and so piling that there shall be
a roof-like slant to the heap, with furnace-like ventilators
opening from it at intervals, I have never found necessary
in actual practice, the elevation of the earth above the
bed being a sufficient water shed, while the cold nature of
the root prevents heating.   Rats are the great enemies of
root pits.   I have had galleries cut by these vermin through
a bed of roots, utterly destroying them for seed purposes.
The best way of killing them in my experience, has been to
drop a little arsenic on buttered bread and put it convenient-
ly near their holes, but so far hidden that no neighbors dog
would be likely to suffer by it.

FEEDING THE CROP.

Besides arguments which are of weight for cultivation of
all kind of roots, there are special ones for the raising of
Mangolds.   The vast bulk of yield exceeds that of any
annual crop, as high as eighty tons of roots having been
raised to the acre on the sewerage farms of England, and
when to this is added the weight of leaves that such a crop
would carry, it will be safe to say that a hundred tons have
been given to the acre.   Taken as a whole the Mangold has
less enemies and is less apt to fail than any other root.
Compared with the Turnip family, it has several marked advantages, being more reliable in dry seasons and less liable
to disease ; and in flesh-forming, heat-giving and fat-produc-
ing elements it surpasses it.   While the Turnip family cannot
be raised repeatedly on the same land, indeed on most soil
can be raised only at intervals of three or four years, Mangolds can be raised many years in succession, as Mr. Mechi,
the distinguished English agriculturist, has proved by raising
sixty tons per annum on the same tract of land of six acres
area, for six successive years.   They will keep longer in good

condition than any other root, under favorable circumstances even as late as July. Experiments in feeding steers made with care, proved that while a ton of Mangolds increased their weight sixty five pounds, a ton of Swede increased their weight but forty-eight pounds, equal quantities of hay having been fed in each experiment. Other experiments have established about the same proportionate value between these two roots, though the general result was not as favorable. Mangolds, like fruit, undergo a ripening change after they are gathered, and until this is effected they are not in the best condition for feeding. The ripening process for the most part consists in a change of starch into sugar, and makes the Mangolds both more healthful and more nutritious food. Before this change is effected they are apt to scour stock if fed to any degree liberally. The time when this chemical change takes place will depend on the degree of ripeness of the crop when stored ; and this, as has been clearly shown is affected by both the soil on which they grew and the manure with which they were fed ; other conditions equal, those grown on upland ripen earlier than those on lowland, while rank manures tend to prolong the period of growth and crops so grown, come into condition for feeding later in the season. In England, a common practice is to begin feeding the Mangolds at Christmas, while in this country the middle of January is considered early enough. Experiments carefully made have proved that when fed to fattening animals they should follow and not precede Turnips. It is a good rule in feeding this as with other roots or tubers, to begin with a small quantity and gradually increase the amount up to the limit which the appetite of the cow, her general health and the tale of the milk pail indicates. Every farmer who feeds a dairy needs a root cutter. There are several of these in the market, some designed for sheep only, which cut the roots into small pieces, others for neat cattle, while some manufactured by our Canada neighbors can be arranged to cut for either class of stock. As good a one as I know of for stock purposes, cheapness, durability and effectiveness combined, is one sometimes known as the Whittemore machine, of which I present an engraving. This machine is capable of cutting

about two bushels a minute. Experiments in England have shown that 59 pounds of cooked Mangolds are equal to 70 of uncooked; but that meat made from steamed food wastes more when boiled. Leaves of Mangolds should be fed with care as they are more apt to scour than those of any other root. The reason

WHITTEMORE CUTTER.

of this is that they contain comparatively a large quantity of a poisonous acid, known by chemists as "oxalic" acid, the same that is developed in Rhubarb leaves, when slightly wilted, and which sometimes causes death when such leaves are eaten as "greens."

The practice sometimes followed in Europe, of feeding the leaves of the growing crop, where labor is very cheap, is thought to pay, as the leaves are gathered just as they begin to drop from their upright position and when their usefulness as nourishers of the root have ended. But with labor as cheap as may be, there is no economy in this, for, aside from the deleterious effects to animals, when fed too liberally, by actual experiment it has been found that the wear and tear to the crop, incidental to the plucking of these leaves by an average farm hand, injures it more than the value of the leaves after they are gathered.

Were it not for the enormous bulk that an acre will produce in roots when compared with its yield in hay or grain, there would be a serious argument against the growing of them to any extent beyond what might be needed for medicinal purposes, in the fact that the manure made from them is of so low a value ; and the practical weight of this argument would grow in proportion as farmers acquire a knowledge of the most important department of farming. To most farmers a cord or load of manure of cow or horse is a cord or load of equal value ; now this is far, very far from being the fact, as will be seen by the following table which I take from the *Scientific Farmer*, compiled by the celebrated Mr. Lewis, who, by his careful experiments has laid the agricultural world under lasting obligation. In this table a ton of English hay is taken as the standard, and were all the manure saved, both solid and liquid, from a ton of each of these varieties of food, the ingredients at the market value of the Ammonia, Potash and Phosphoric Acid would be worth as follows :—

Hay,	$10.00
Clover Hay,	15.00
Oat Straw,	4.50
Wheat Straw,	4.16
Barley Straw,	3.50
Decorticated Cotton Seed Cake,	43.33
Linseed Cake,	30.66
Malt Dust,	28.33
Malt,	10.50

Oats, - - - - - -	11.50
Wheat, . - - - -	11.00
Indian Corn, - - - - -	10.50
Barley, - - - - - -	9.83
Potatoes, - - - - -	2.33
Mangolds, - - - - - -	1.66
Swedes, - - - - - -	1.41
Turnips, (common,) - - - -	1.33
Carrots, - - - - - -	1.33

This table is very suggestive in many ways :—by it we see that there are varieties of food, the manure from which is worth more than the cost of the food itself. In its application to the feeding of Mangolds, it at a glance suggests the wisdom of feeding at the same time a portion of something richer and more concentrated. By so doing the quality of the manure is vastly improved and the crops will not be slow to discover it. There is still another reason for feeding these rich foods while using roots ; it enables the armer to feed with profit his straw or inferior varieties of hay. Says Prof. Stockhardt, "the full benefit to animals derivable from feeding roots is secured only when the proper proportion of substances rich in nitrogen are fed with them ; accordingly, about two pounds of oil-cake should be fed with each hundred pounds of beet root, or other foods may be substituted in the same proportion as they are rich in nitrogen."

Recent researches have determined a fact of great value to agriculture ; that to get the most profitable results from food the Albuminoid and Carbohydrate elements should bear a certain proportion to each other, and that while a decrease in either of them from this proper proportion means insufficient food, and a consequent loss of flesh, fat or milk, an excess of either means money wasted. The proportion for cows that are dry and oxen when not at work, is about, one of Albuminoids to eight of Carbohydrates; for oxen at work and cows in milk, one of Albuminoids to from four to six of Carbohydrates.

The following table taken from Prof. Johnson's excellent work, "How Crops Grow," gives the proportion of the Albuminoids, Carbohydrates and other elements in roots and tubers.

	Water.	Organic Matter.	Ash.	Albuminoids	Carbohydrates,	Crude Fibre.	Fat, &c.
ROOTS AND TUBERS.							
POTATO.	95.0	24.1	0.9	2.0	21.0	1.1	0.3
JERUSALEM ARTICHOKE.	80.0	18.9	1.1	2.0	15.6	1.3	0.5
KOHL-RABI.	88.0	10.8	1 2	2.3	7.3	1.2	0.2
FIELD BEETS, (3 lbs. weight).	88.0	11.1	0.9	1.1	9.1	0.9	0.1
SUGAR BEETS. (1 to 2 lbs.)	81.5	17.7	0.8	1.0	15.4	1.3	0.1
RUTA BAGAS, (about 3 lbs.)	87.0	12.0	1.0	1.6	9.3	1.1	0.1
CARROT, (about 1-2 lb.)	85.0	14.0	1.0	1.5	10.8	1.7	0.2
GIANT CARROT. (1 to 2 lbs.)	87.0	12.2	0.8	1.2	9.8	1.2	0.2
TURNIPS.	92.0	7.2	0.8	1.1	5.1	1.0	0.1
PARSNIP.	88.3	11.0	0.7	1.6	8.4	1.0	0.2
PUMPKIN.	94.5	4.5	1.0	1.3	2.8	1.0	0.1

To give the tables necessary to develop this interesting subject to its full capacity, would be altogether beyond the scope of my little treatise. I will refer my readers to the appendix of that excellent work by Prof. Johnson, "How Crops Grow."

THE COST OF THE CROP.

An average crop of Mangolds may be set down at 22 tons. To grow this crop would cost the farmer who depends on barn manure mainly, about as follows :—

DEBTOR.

Ploughing twice, harrowing and dragging, - -	$9.00
Seed,—4 lbs., - - - - -	3.00
Planting, - - - - - -	1.00
Sliding, weeding and thinning crop, - -	16.00
Gathering, topping and storing, - - -	12.00
Manure, and handling of 7 cords, - -	56.00
Refuse salt, 16 bushels, at $1.25 per hogshead, -	2.50
Interest, taxes and wear and tear of implements and teams, - - - - -	15.00

Total cost, $114.50

CREDITOR.

By crop of 22 tons roots, at $8.50 per ton, -	$187.00
" tops,—4 tons, at $5.00, - - -	20.00
" value of manure left in soil, - -	14.00

$221.00

114.50

Balance, $106.50

In the above estimate I have assumed most of the labor to be by boys, who at hand weeding, if they are reliable, can get over the ground faster than men. I have made no allowance for the cost of cutting up the roots when feeding, as this does not belong under this head. Should the land be old the item of weeding would have to be increased one-half. The salt I have priced at its cost along the sea-coast. I have estimated the value of the crop at the average value of several years past, while the manure charge is much higher than it should be where farmers have access to the fertilizing wastes of great cities.

Now, if instead of being contented with a crop of 22 tons to the acre, the farmer strives for double that quantity, he will get it by additional expense in but two directions, viz. : his manure bill and the cost of gathering and storing. If we now double the cost of each of the latter, and credit the results with double the crop, which every practical farmer who has had experience in root culture will allow is but reasonable, we shall have the following results :—

Extra cost of crop of 44 tons over one of 22 :

Manure,—7 cords,	-	-	-	$56.00
Gathering, topping and storing,	-	-	-	12.00
				$68.00

Now adding the credit side we shall have for

Extra 22 tons roots,	-	-	-	$187.00
6 tons tops,	-	-	-	30.00
Value of manure left in ground,	-	-	-	14.00
				$231.00
Deduct extra cost,				68.00
Profits cleared,				$163.00

In other words, by investing $68.00 for six months, we clear $163.00, which, as any farmer boy can figure, is at the rate of about five hundred per cent. a year. Mr. Fearing of Hingham, with the same amount of manure raised over sixty tons to the acre, and the instances are numerous where over forty tons have been the crop when even a less quantity has been used. Can any farmer who has accumulated a small surplus of money do better than invest it in manure? There is altogether too much money, for the prosperity of their farming, invested by farmers in Savings Banks. These banks pay from six to seven per cent. on money, but here is an instance where an investment made in manure pays over four hundred

per cent.   Merchants don't do so foolish a thing as to put
their earnings into Savings Banks.   No ; they invest in their
business and so keep it and its money making capacity under their own control ; when will farmers be as wise and become their own bankers?   Let me remark that the farmer
who is so wise as to attempt to get the most from his
land will do well to follow Prof. Voelcker's advice and drill
in four or five hundred weight of some good phosphate, to
the acre, in place of the same value in stable manure.

In the above estimates of the value of Mangolds we have
assumed that the farmer sold his crop.   Now it is true of this
as of every other crop that the farmer can use on his premises, that it is of more value to him than the general market
price indicates.

Under this head an intelligent farmer of large experience writes :—

"From experiments made in feeding beets, their practical value has been made to range from 13 to 20 cents per
bushel, with hay at twenty dollars per ton.   An exact estimate of the practical value of beets for cattle food, is a difficult matter, as it is now, and ever will be, hid from mortal
ken.   The improved condition of the cow, (when fed to
cows during the winter,) her increased usefulness during the
entire season, her lessened liability to sickness and disease
which high feeding with any one of the different kinds of
grain induces, her lengthened lease of life, her evident satis-
faction and perfect contentment, which is so plainly mani-
fested while eating her daily ration of roots, are each and
every one legitimate items to be taken into the account in
estimating the practical, the actual value of beets as food
for dairy stock.

"After carefully looking at the subject in all its bear-
ings, so far as my experience has given me opportunity to
do so, I have come to the conclusion that beets for cattle

food are well worth fully as many cents per bushel as good hay is worth dollars per ton, without taking into consideration the increase of the manure ; and that the average cost, when stored in the cellar or put into pits, with every item of expense included, need not exceed eight cents per bushel."

I will close my little treatise by remarking that while I cannot expect to have exhausted so prolific a subject, yet I hope and trust that it may prove of value as a guide and a stimulus to some of my many friends in the great community of farmers.

CONTENTS.

		Page.
The Argument for the Raising of Roots,	-	3
THE CARROT	- - - -	5
The Location and Soil	- - -	6
The Manure and its Application	- -	7
Preparing the Bed	- - - -	12
When to Plant	- - - -	13
The Seed and the Planting of it	- -	14
Quantity to the Acre	- - -	15
Varieties, and What Kinds to Grow	- -	17
Early Very Short Scarlet	- -	19
Early Short Scarlet Horn	- -	19
Short Horn	- - - -	19
Danvers Carrot	- - - -	19
Long Orange, or Long Surry	- -	20
Altringham	- - - -	21
Large White Belgian	- - -	21
The Cultivation, and the Impliments needed	-	22
Gathering and Storing the Crop	- -	24
Raising Carrots with Onions	- - -	27
Marketing and Feeding	- - -	28
THE MANGOLD WURTZELS	- -	30
Varieties	- - - - -	32

The Long Varieties   -   -   -   -   32

The Round Varieties   -   -   -   -   33

The Ovoid Varieties   -   -   -   -   33

What Kinds to Grow   -   -   -   -   33

The Soil and its Preparation   -   -   -   36

The Manure and its Application   -   -   37

Salt as an Auxiliary Manure   -   -   -   45

Planting the Seed and Tending the Crop   -   46

Gathering and Storing the Crop   -   -   49

Feeding the Crop   -   -   -   -   52

The Cost of the Crop   -   -   -   57

www.ingramcontent.com/pod-product-compliance
Lightning Source LLC
Chambersburg PA
CBHW021629270326
41931CB00008B/934